Willy Weasely's COLORING BOOK

Copyright © Rick Keene 2020
Willy Weasely Comics and Coloring Book By Rick Keene
On Instagram: arkaygraphix

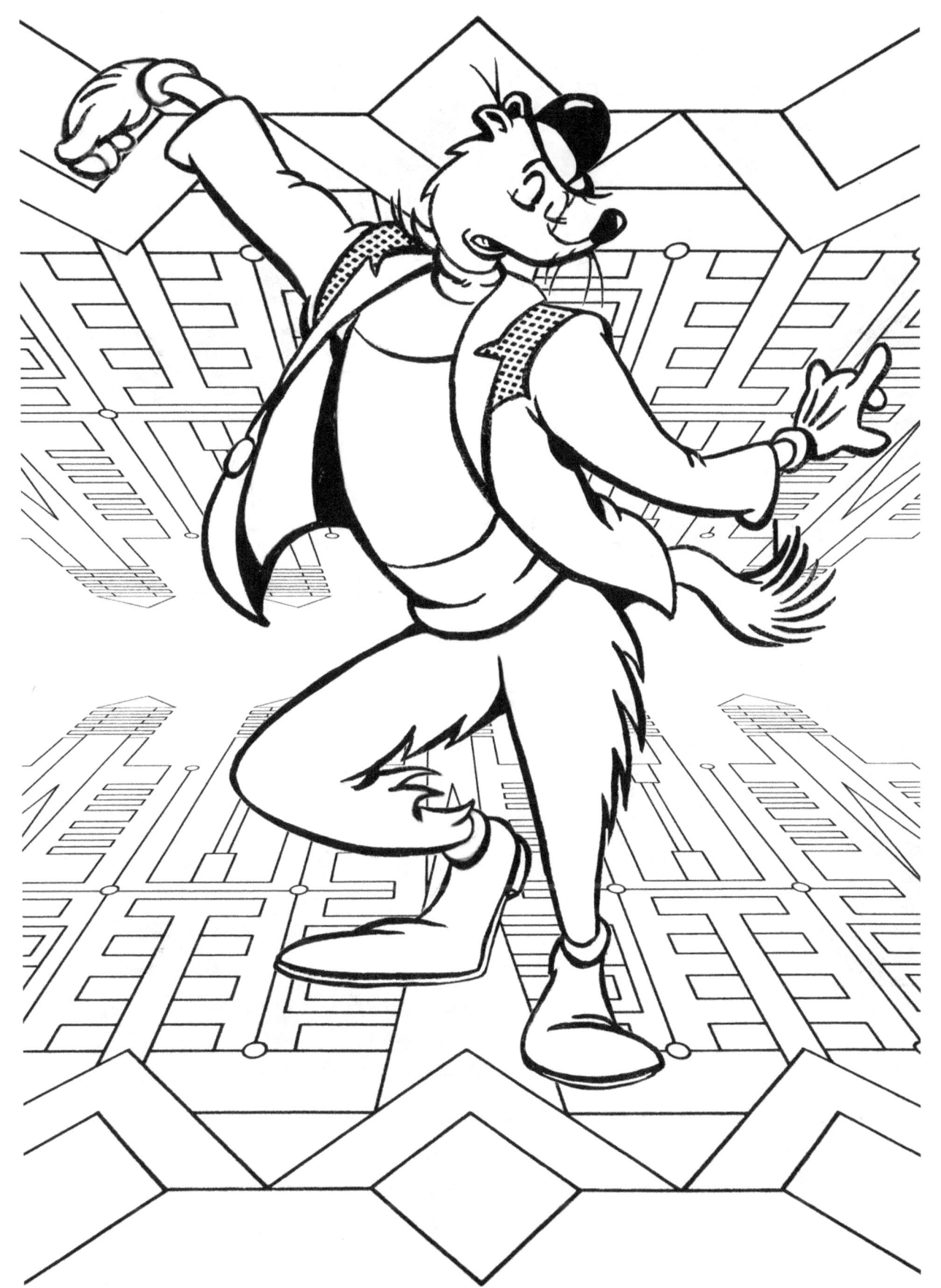

LET'S DANCE

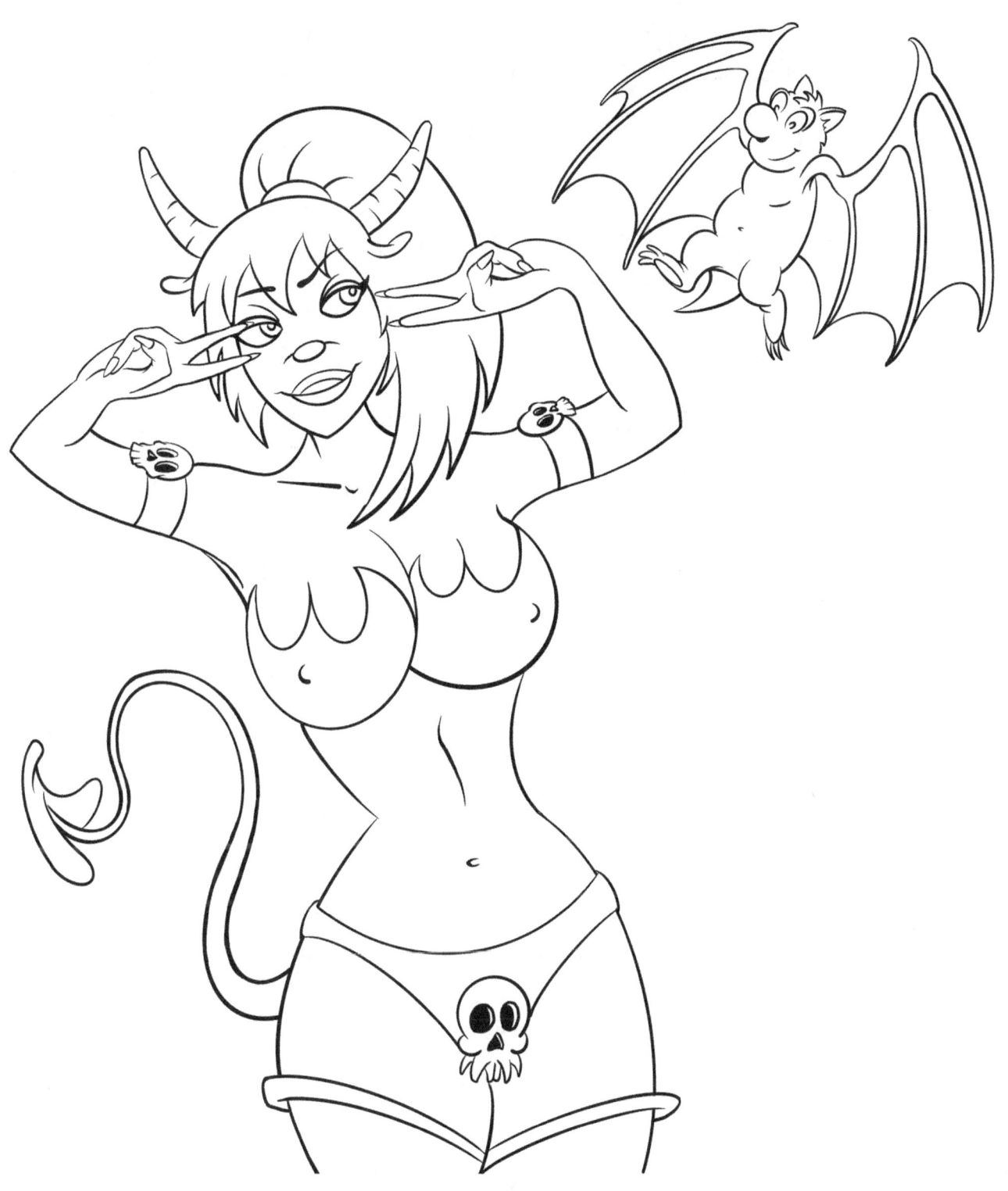

BATUSI

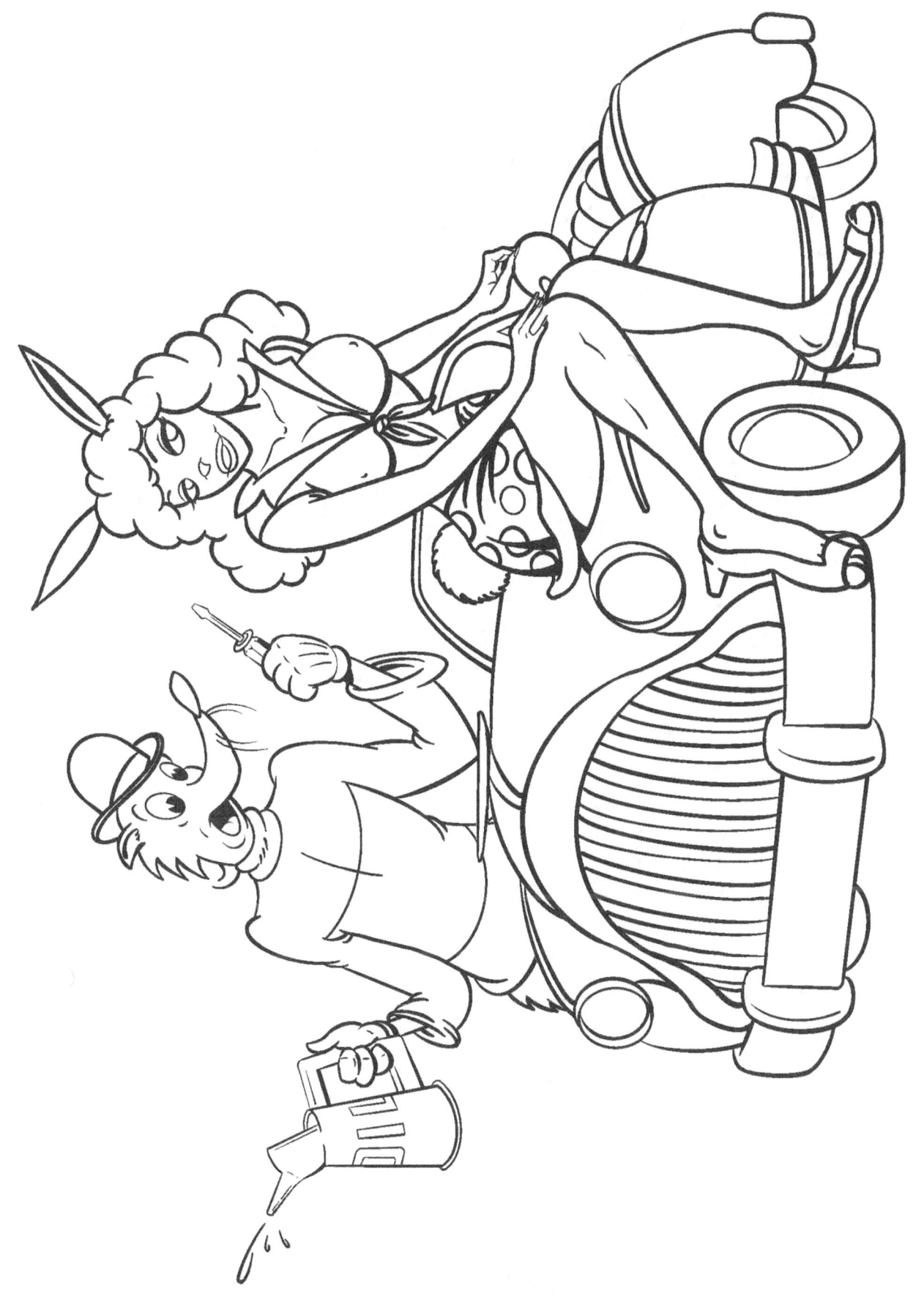

TUNE UP?

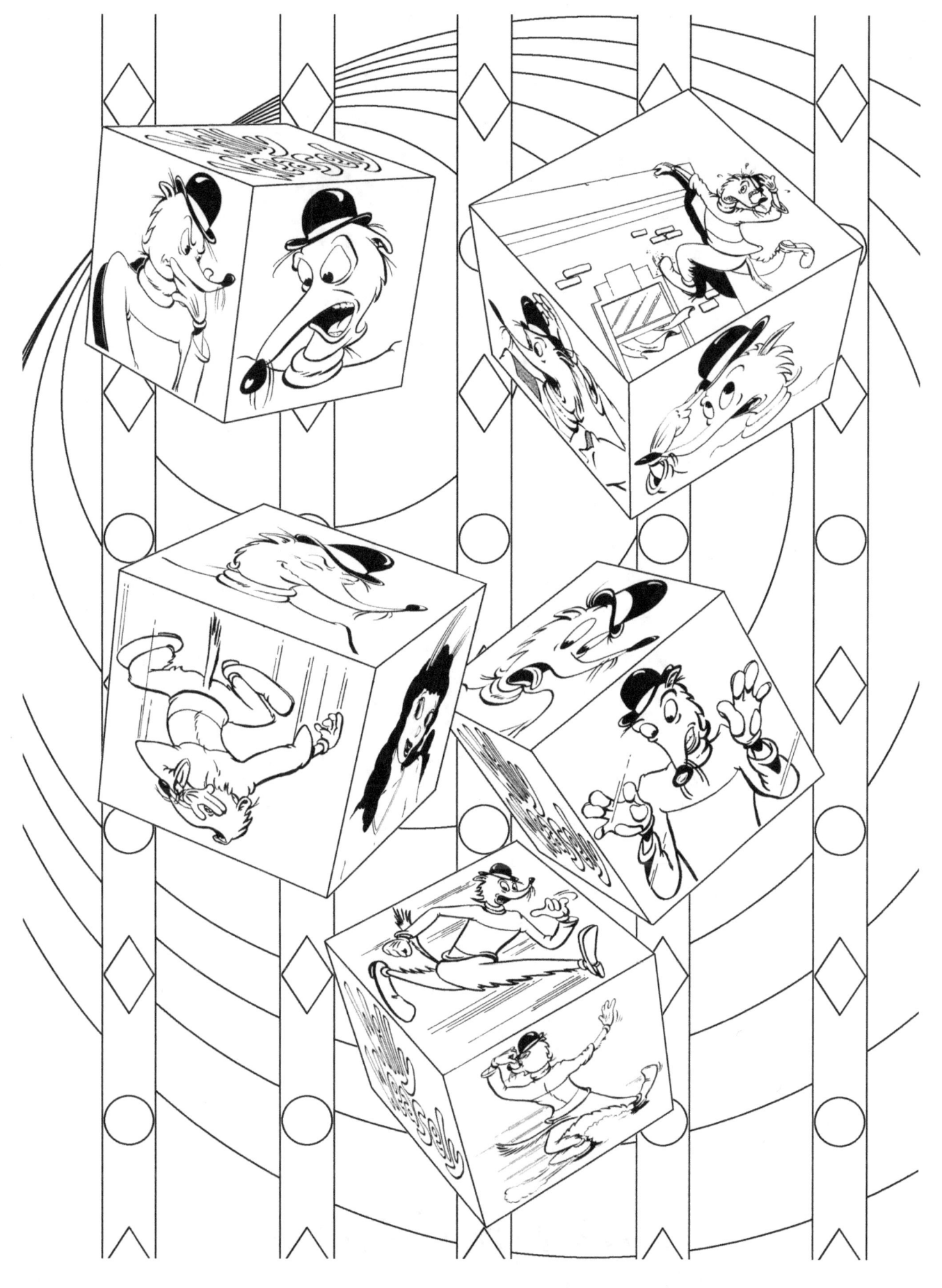

WILLY'S CUBES

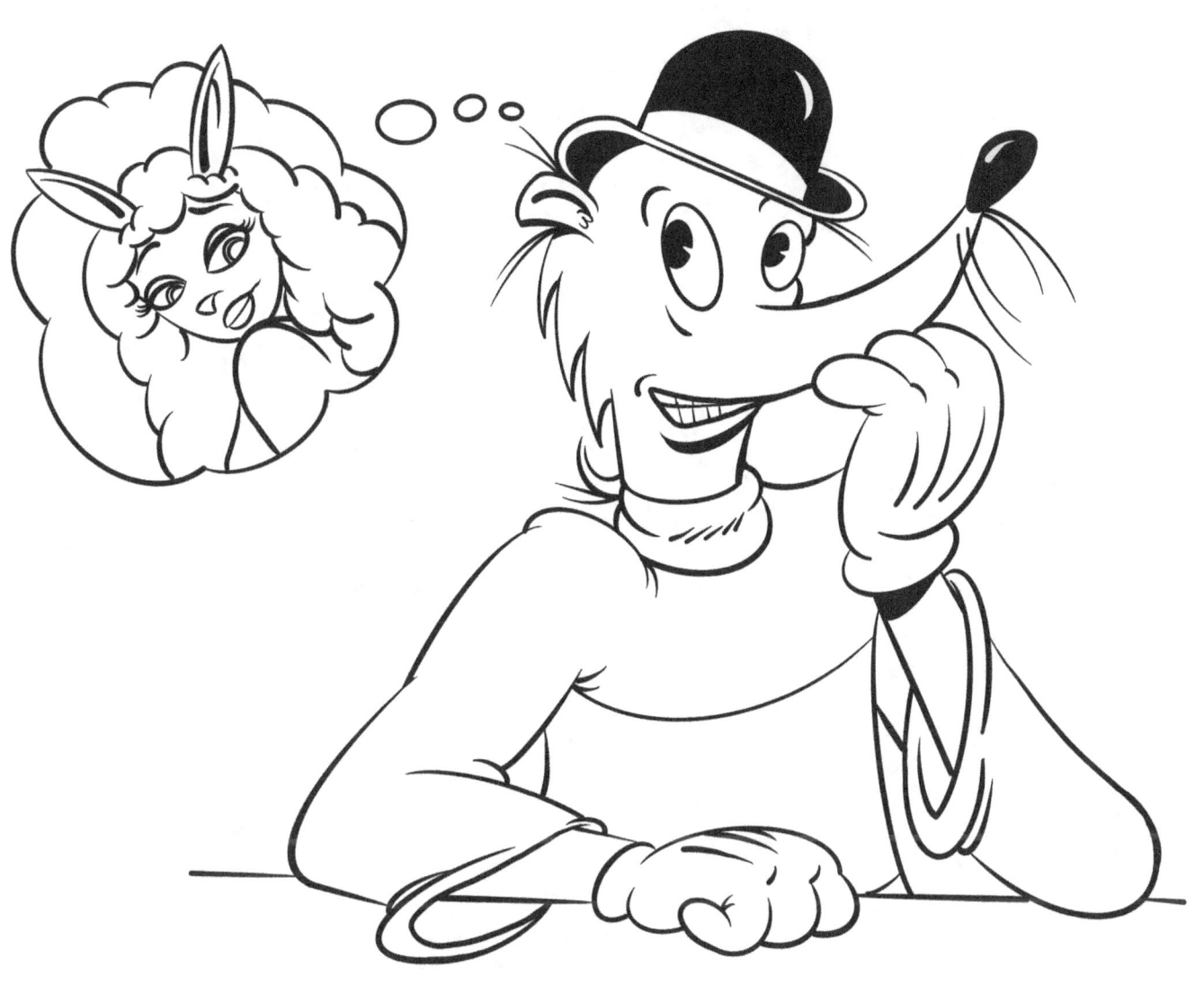

DREAMING OF BUNNY

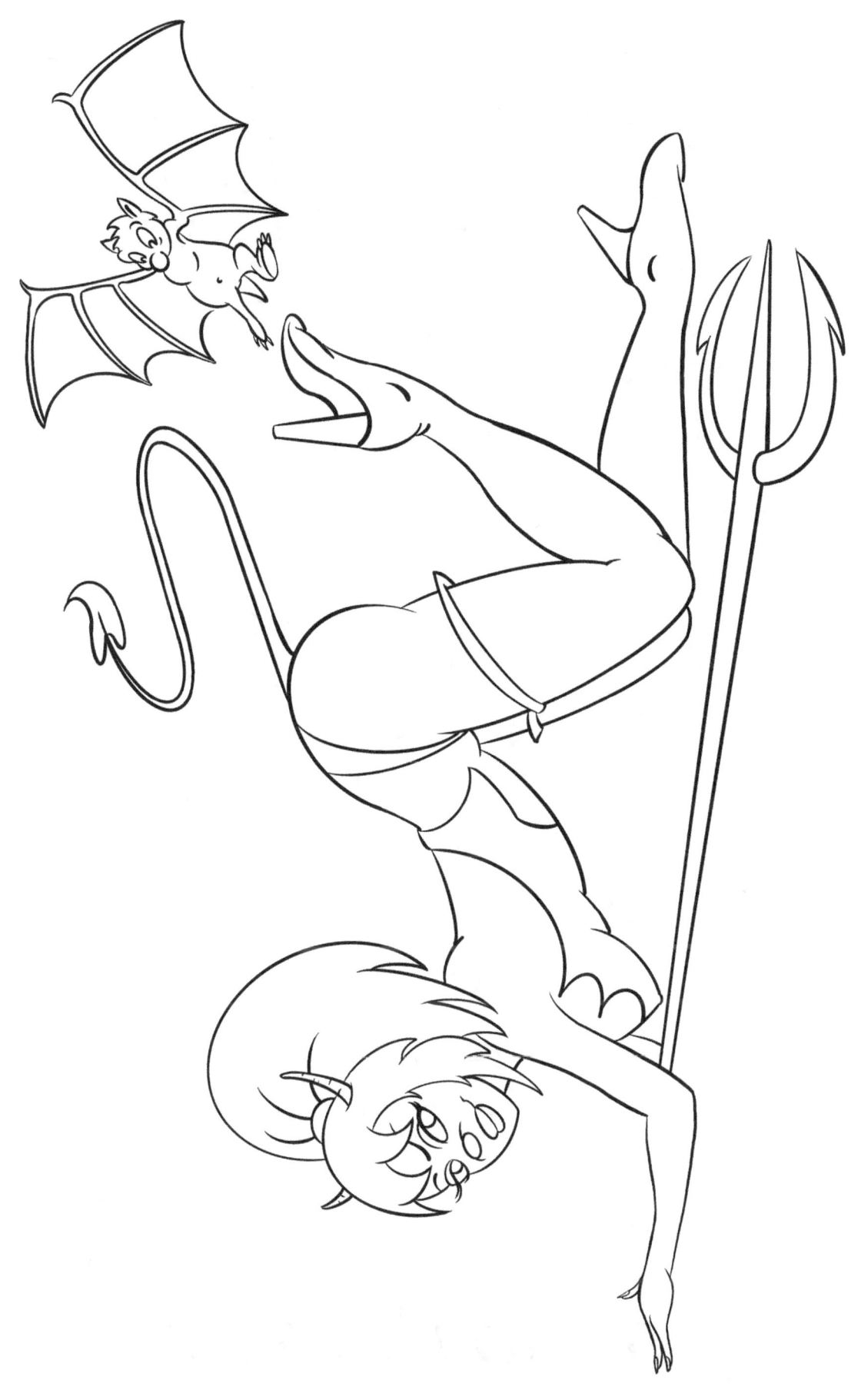

DID YOU TRIP ME?

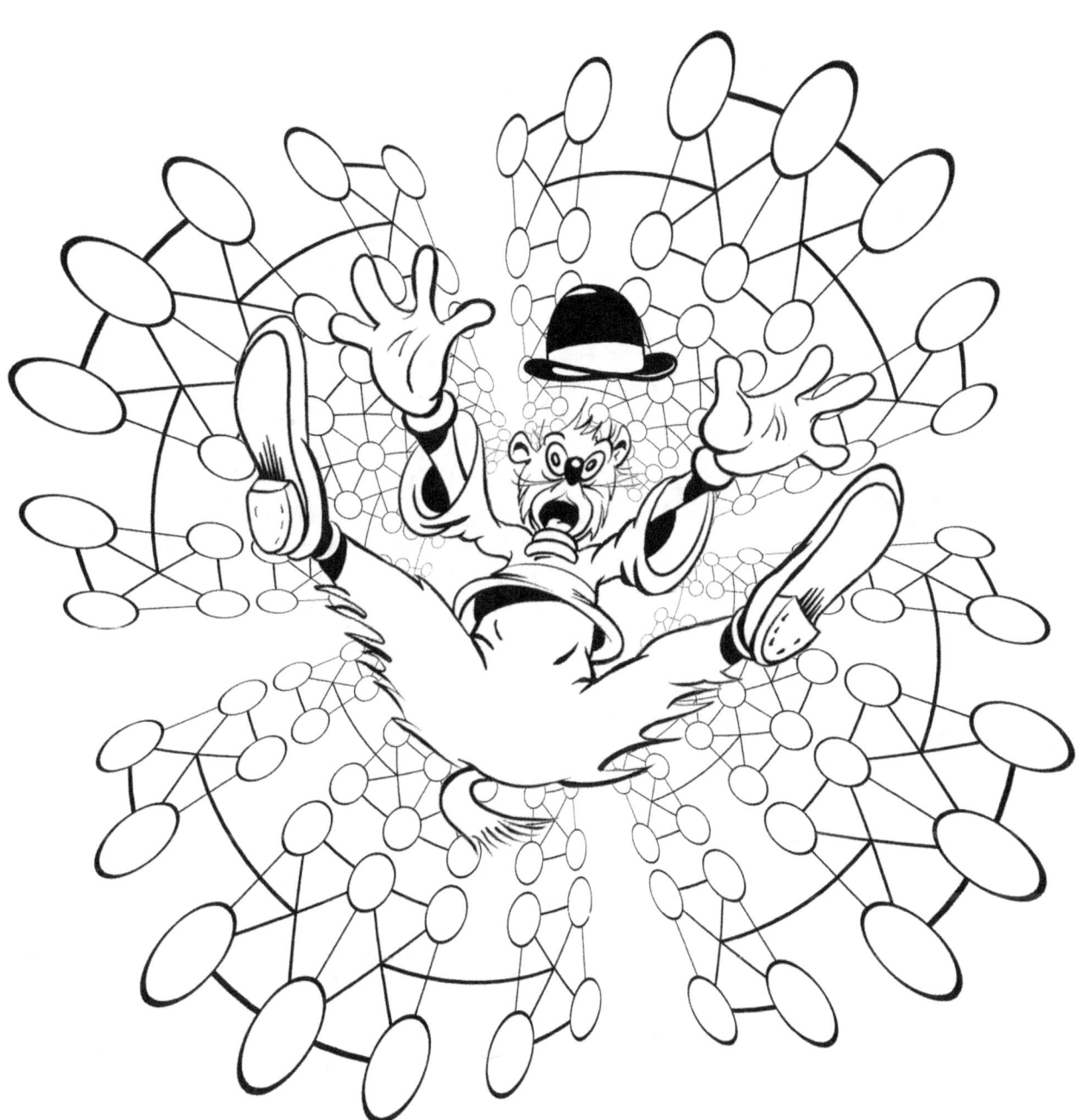

FLUSHED!

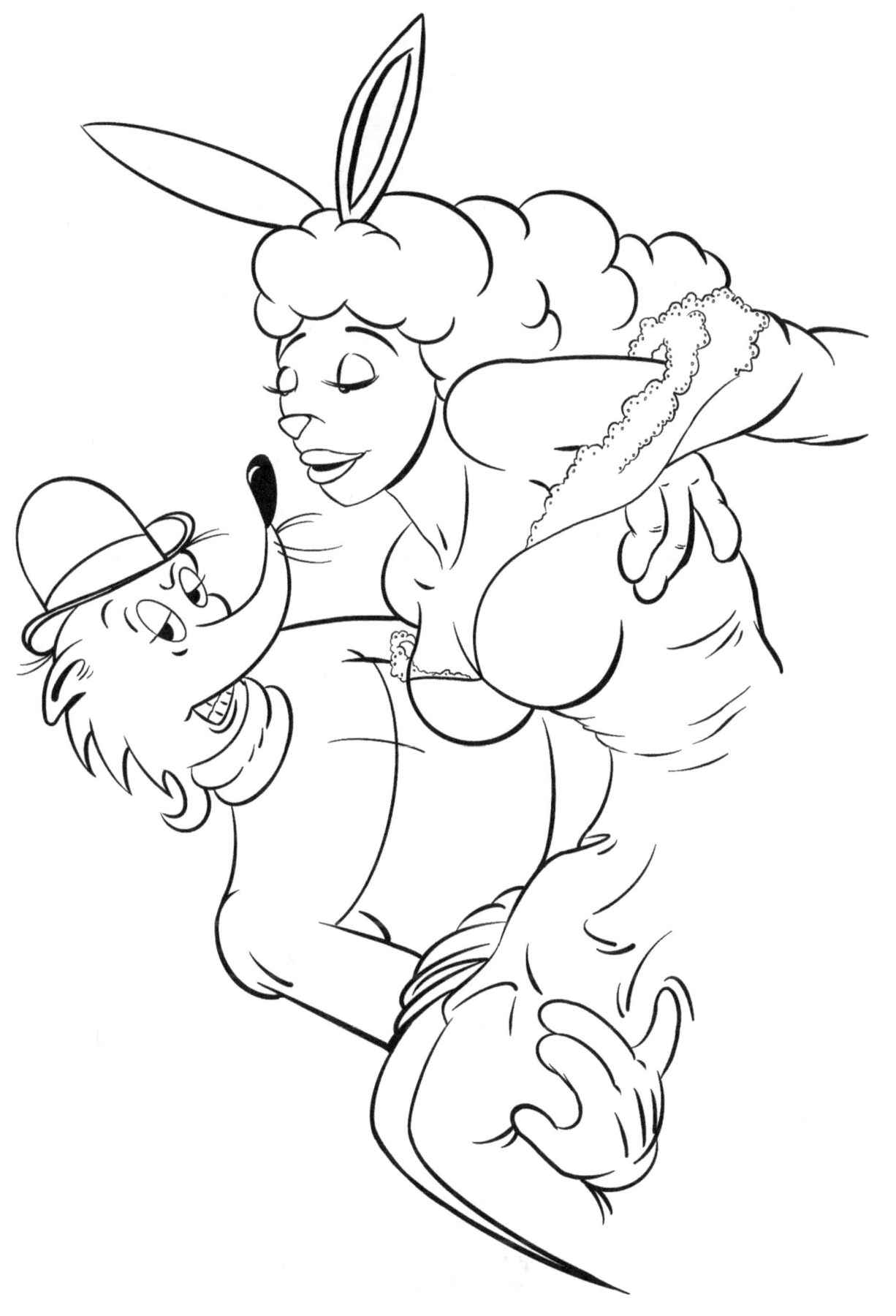

DREAM ON

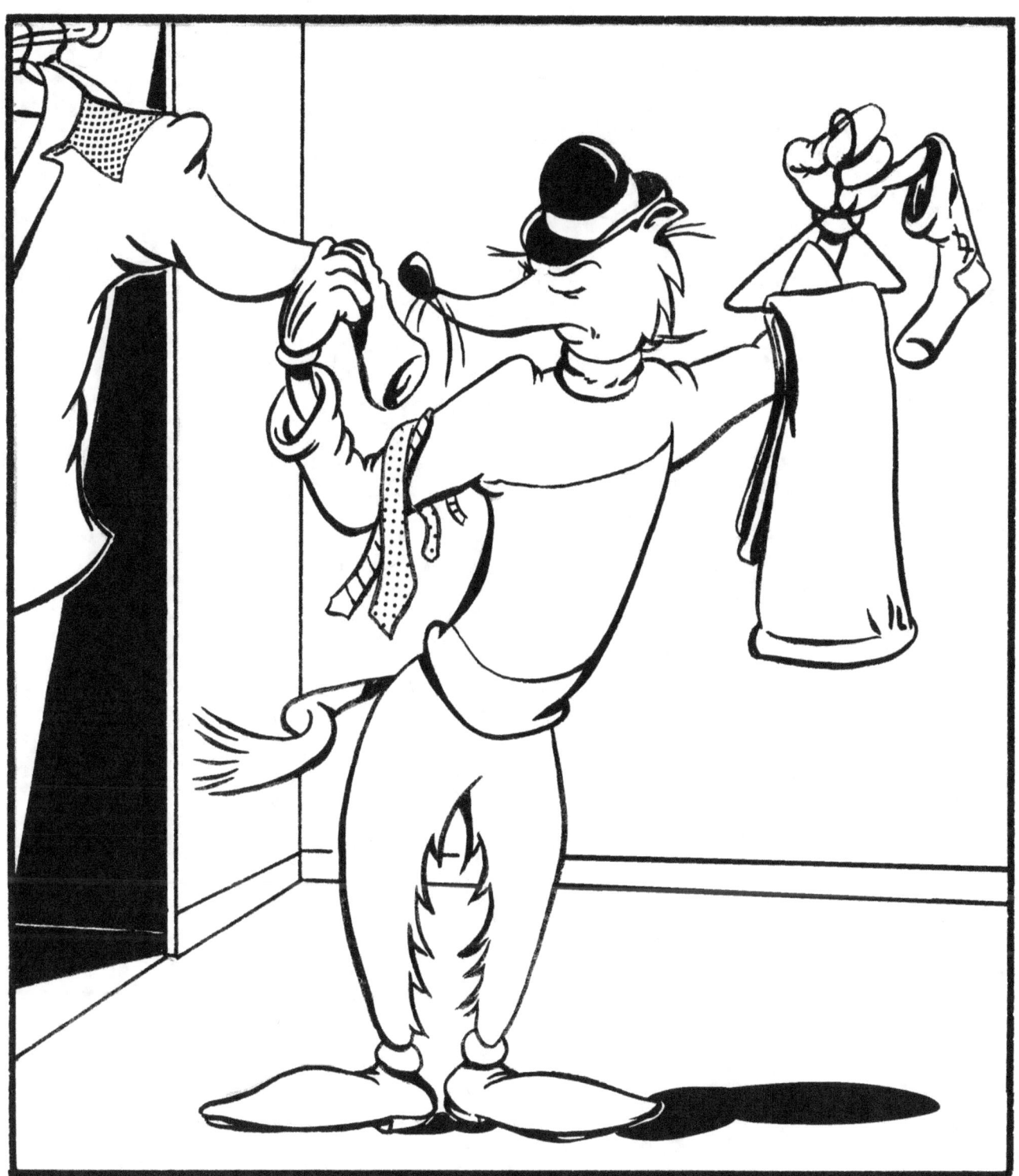

IS POLYESTER STILL IN?

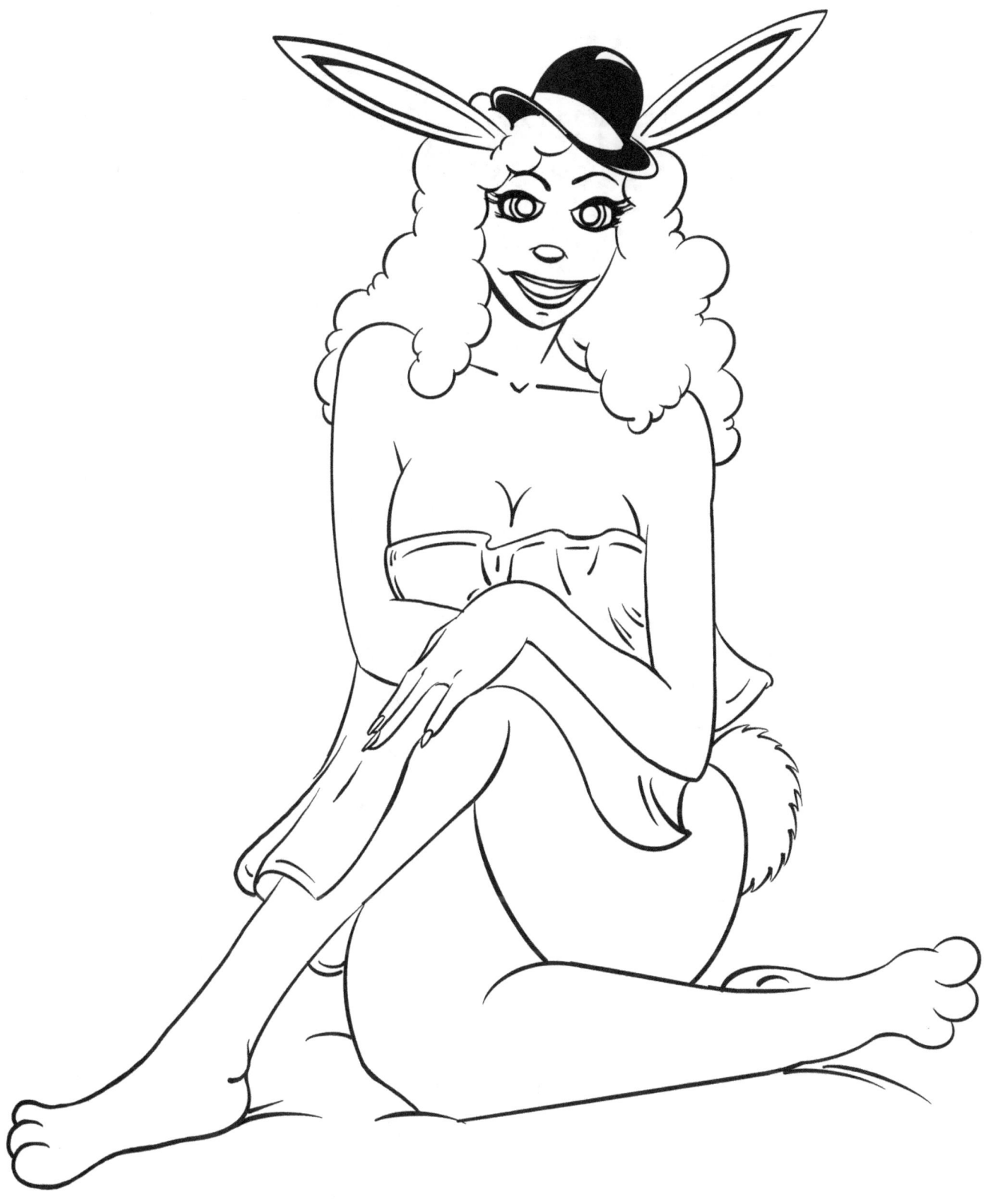

A HAT, A TOWEL, AND A SMILE

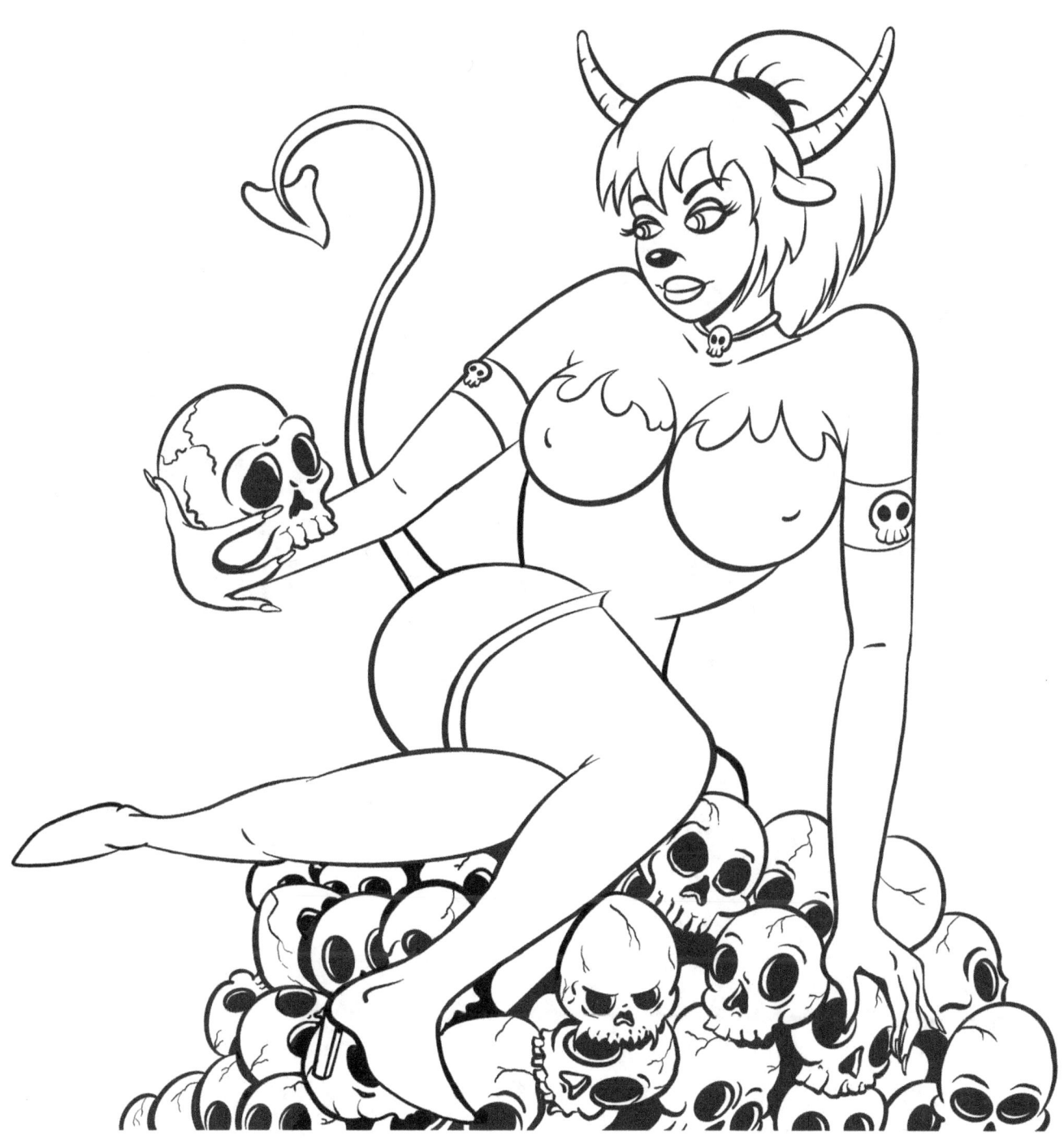

ALAS...

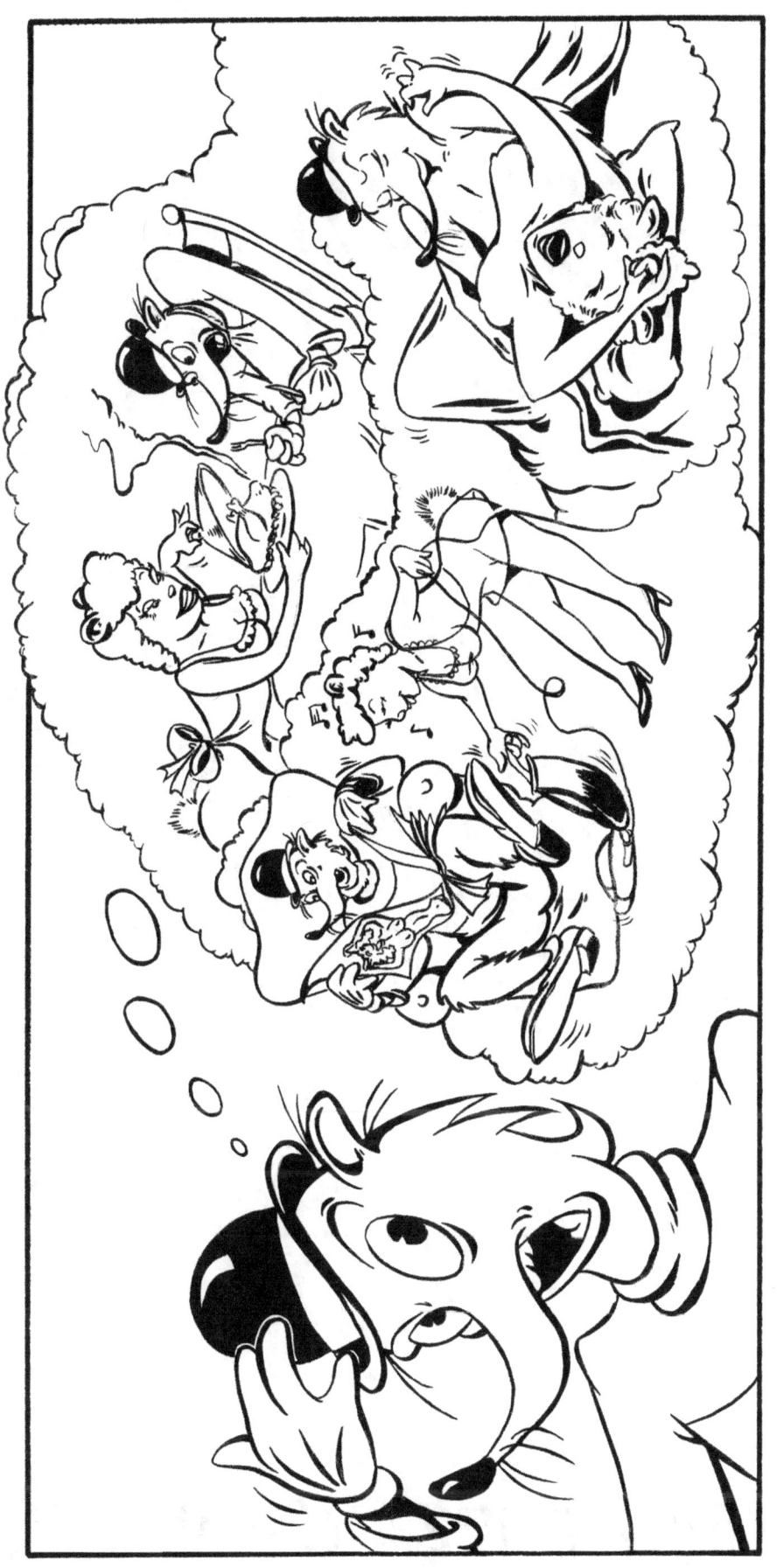

WILLY'S IDEA OF MARRIAGE

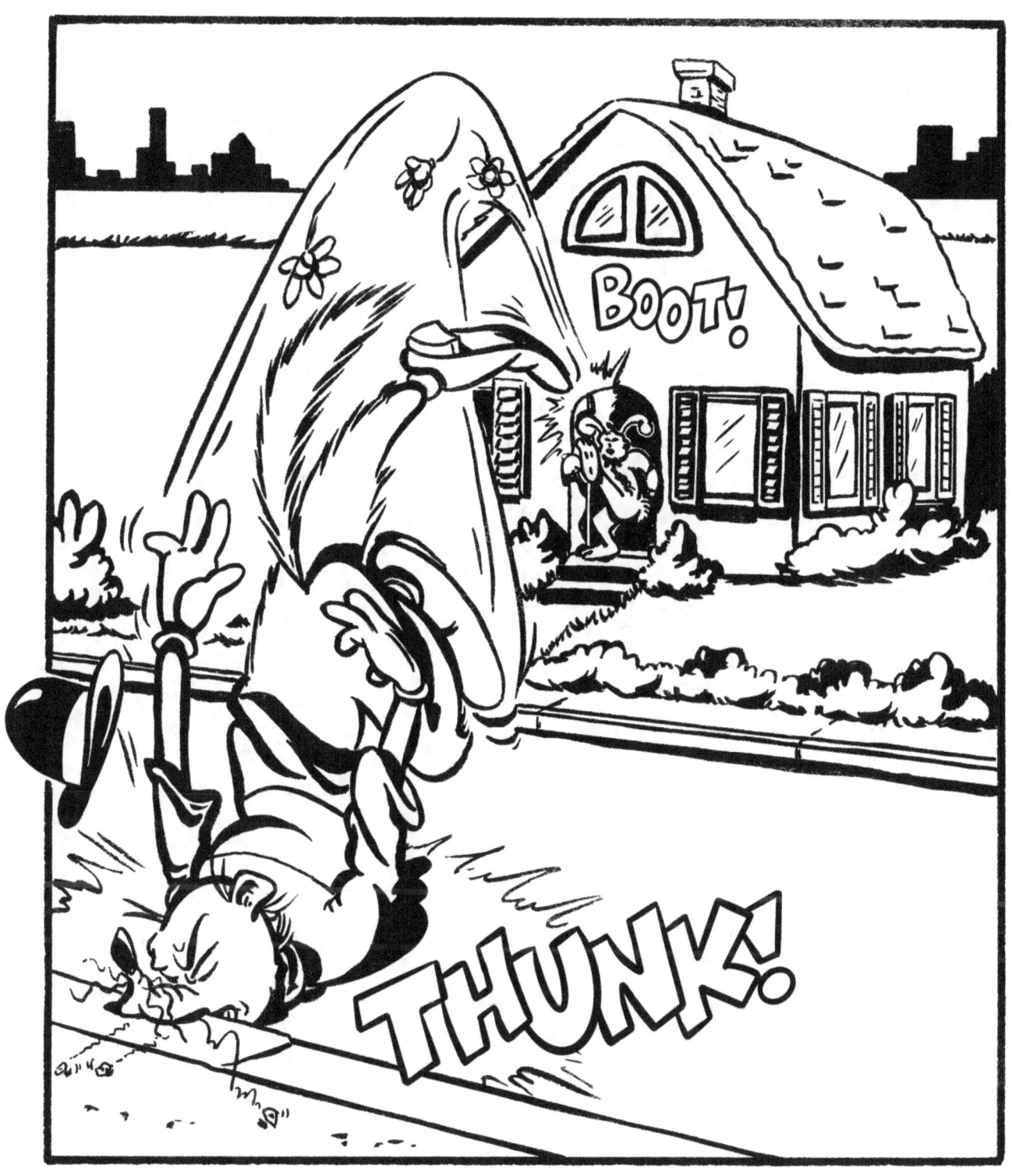

ANOTHER SATISFIED FATHER

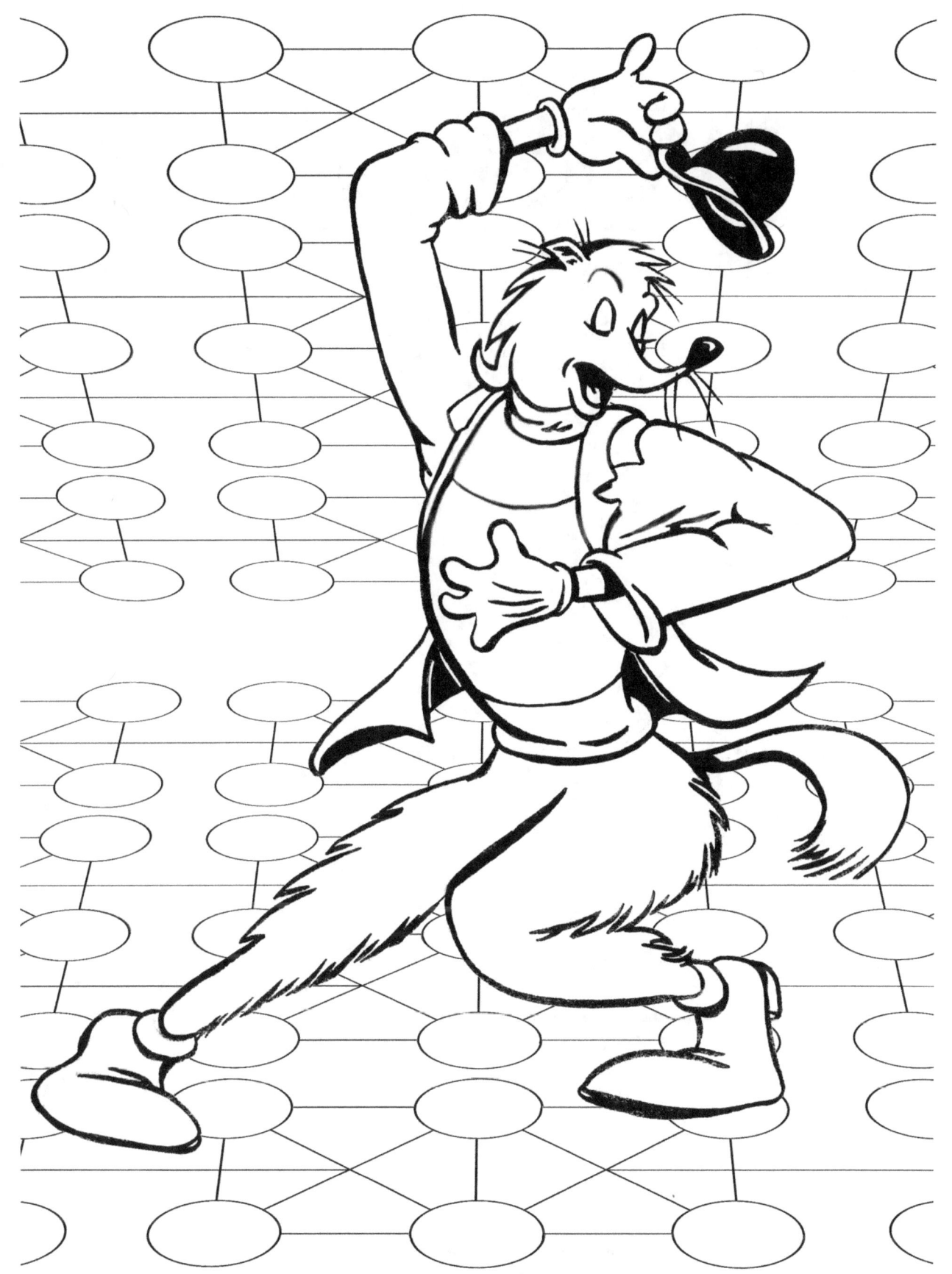

OOH YEAH!

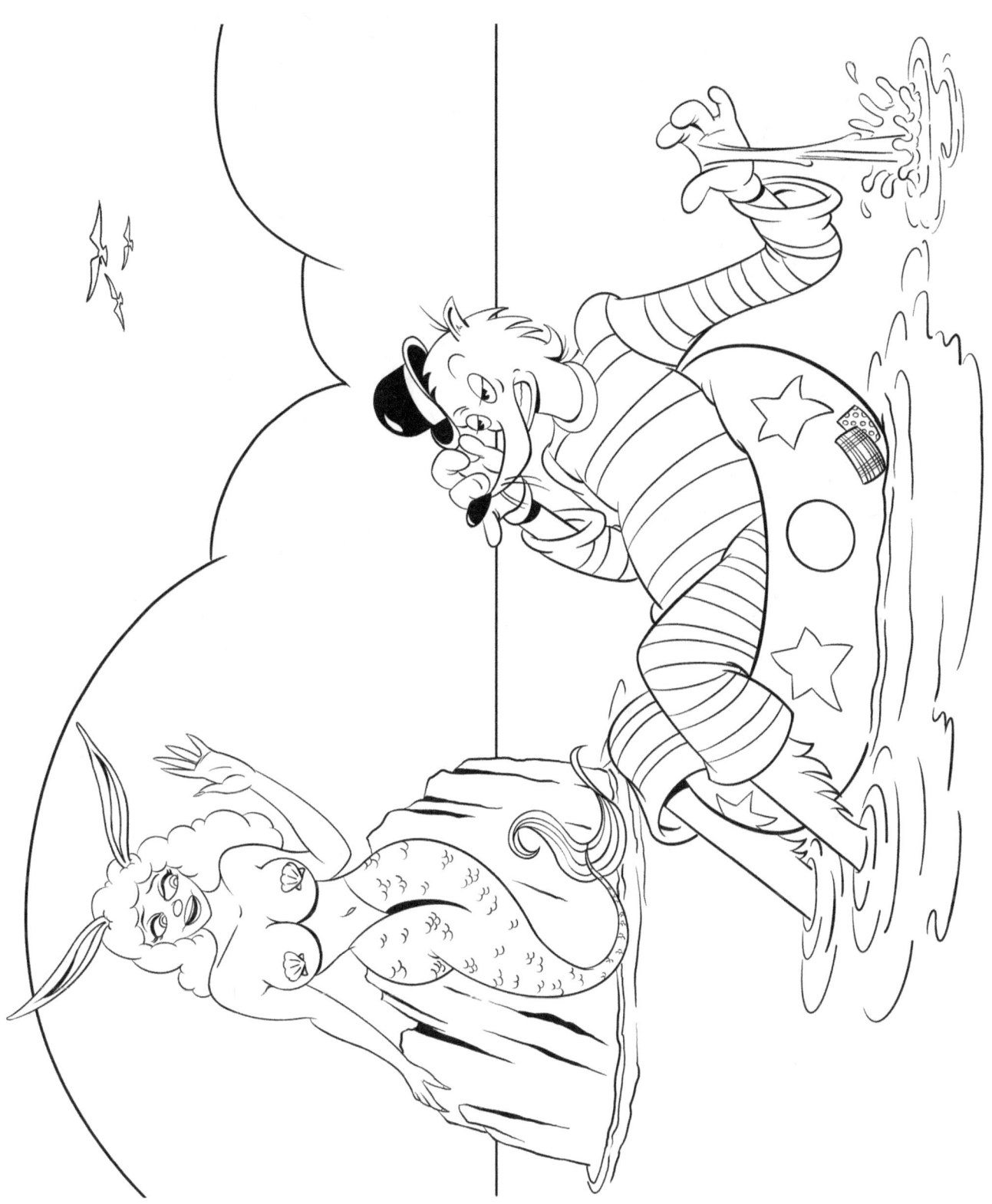

JOIN THE DRIP FOR A DIP?

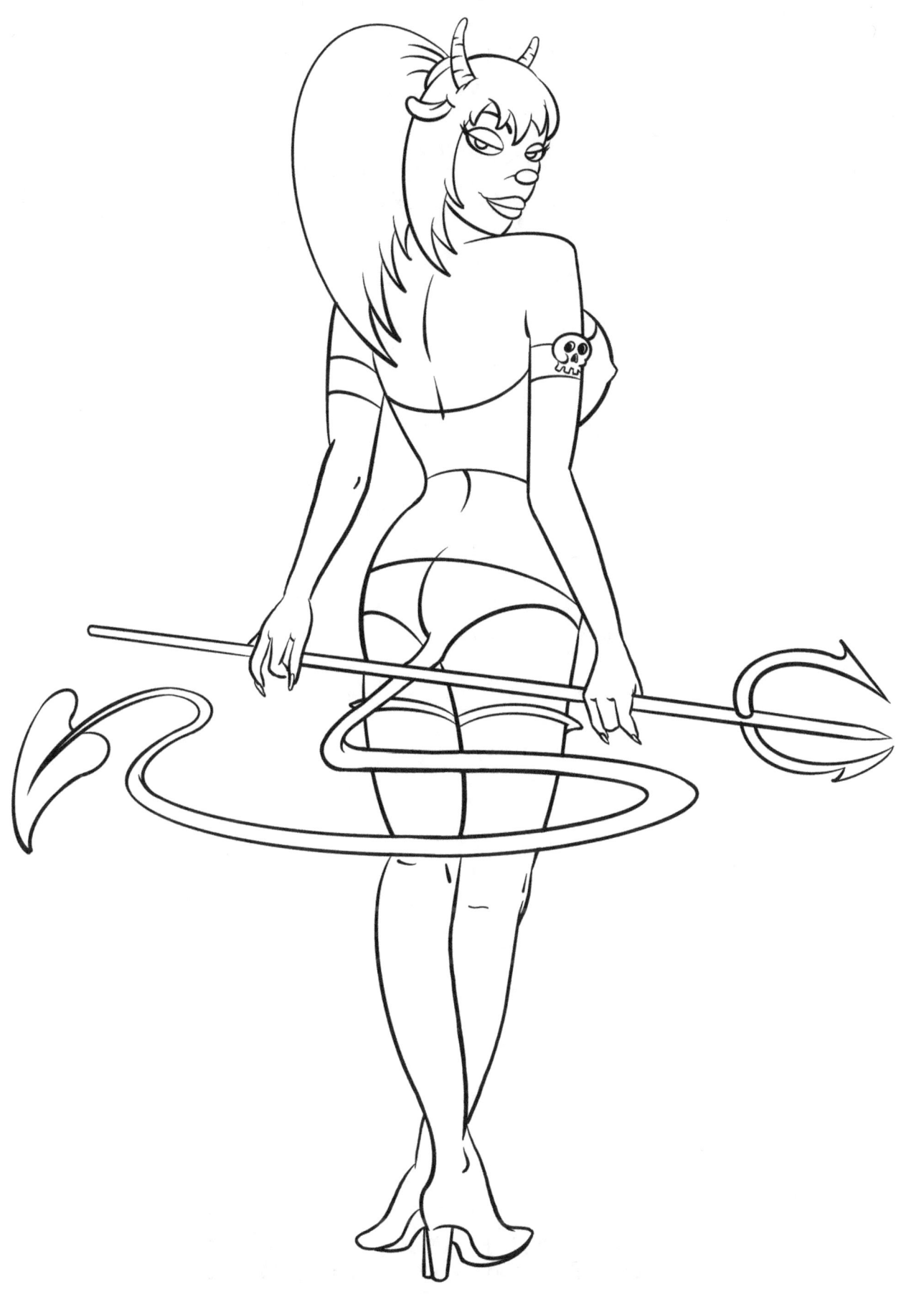

DID YOU CALL ME?

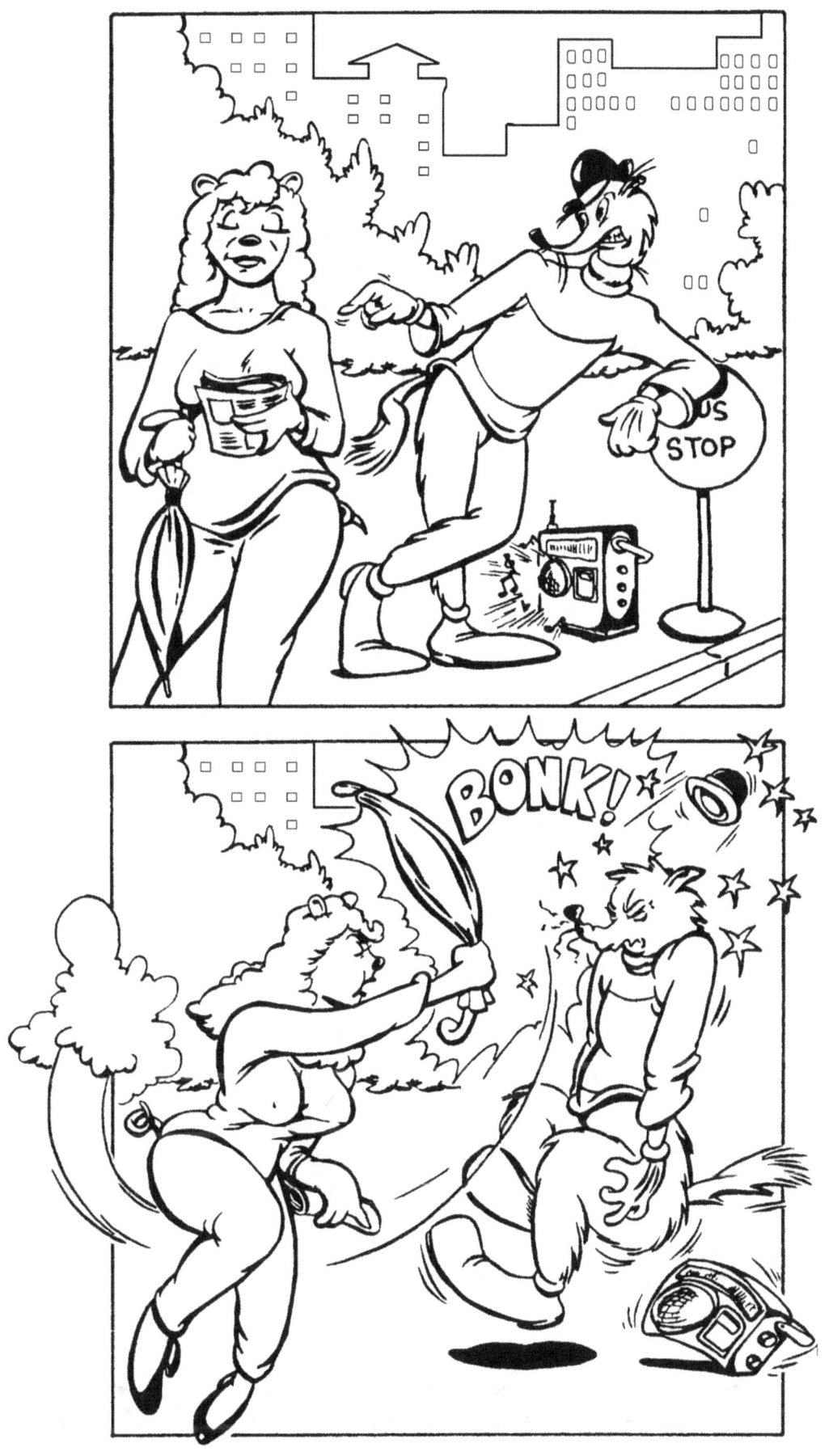

ONE DAY AT THE BUS STOP

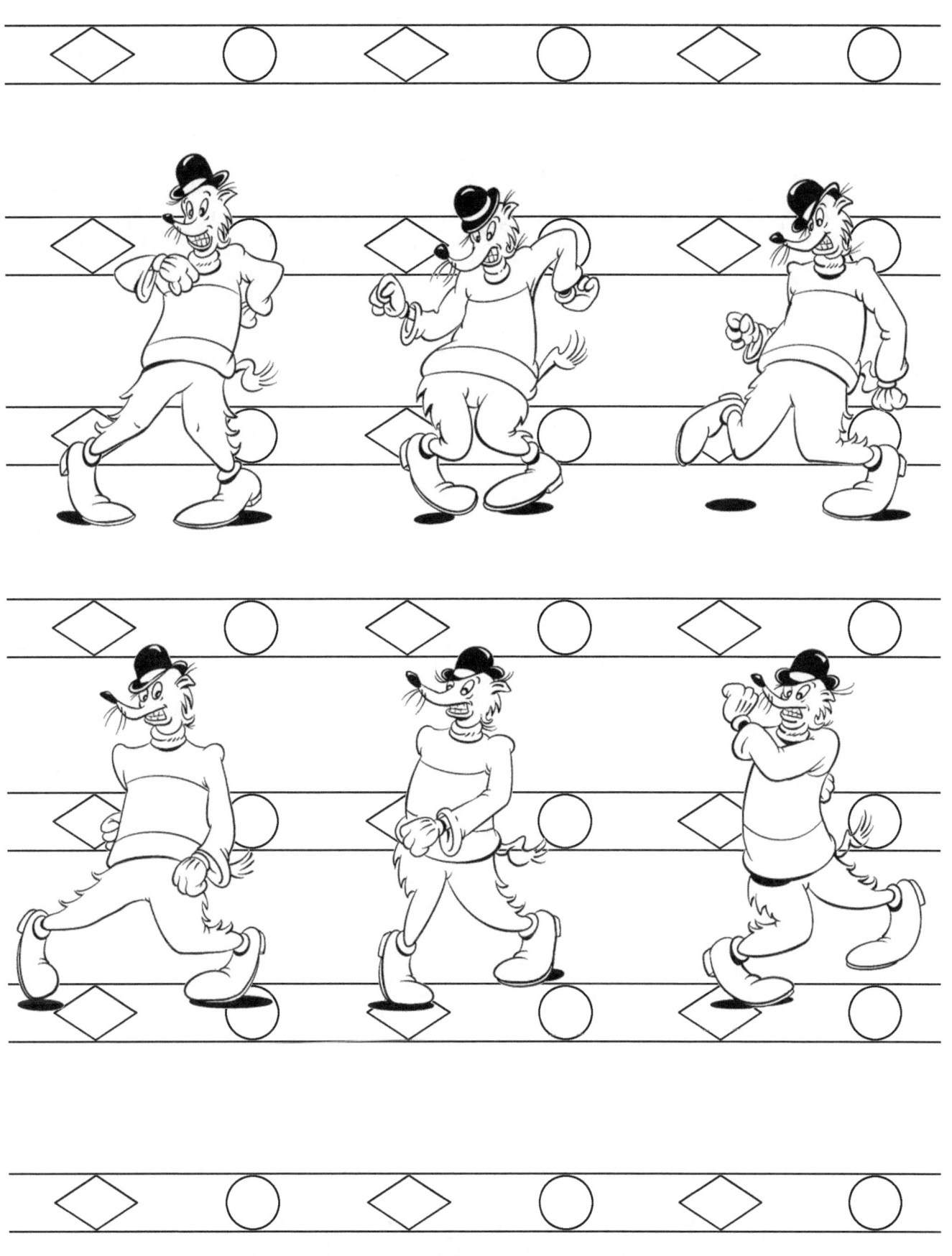

WILLY'S DANCE MOVES

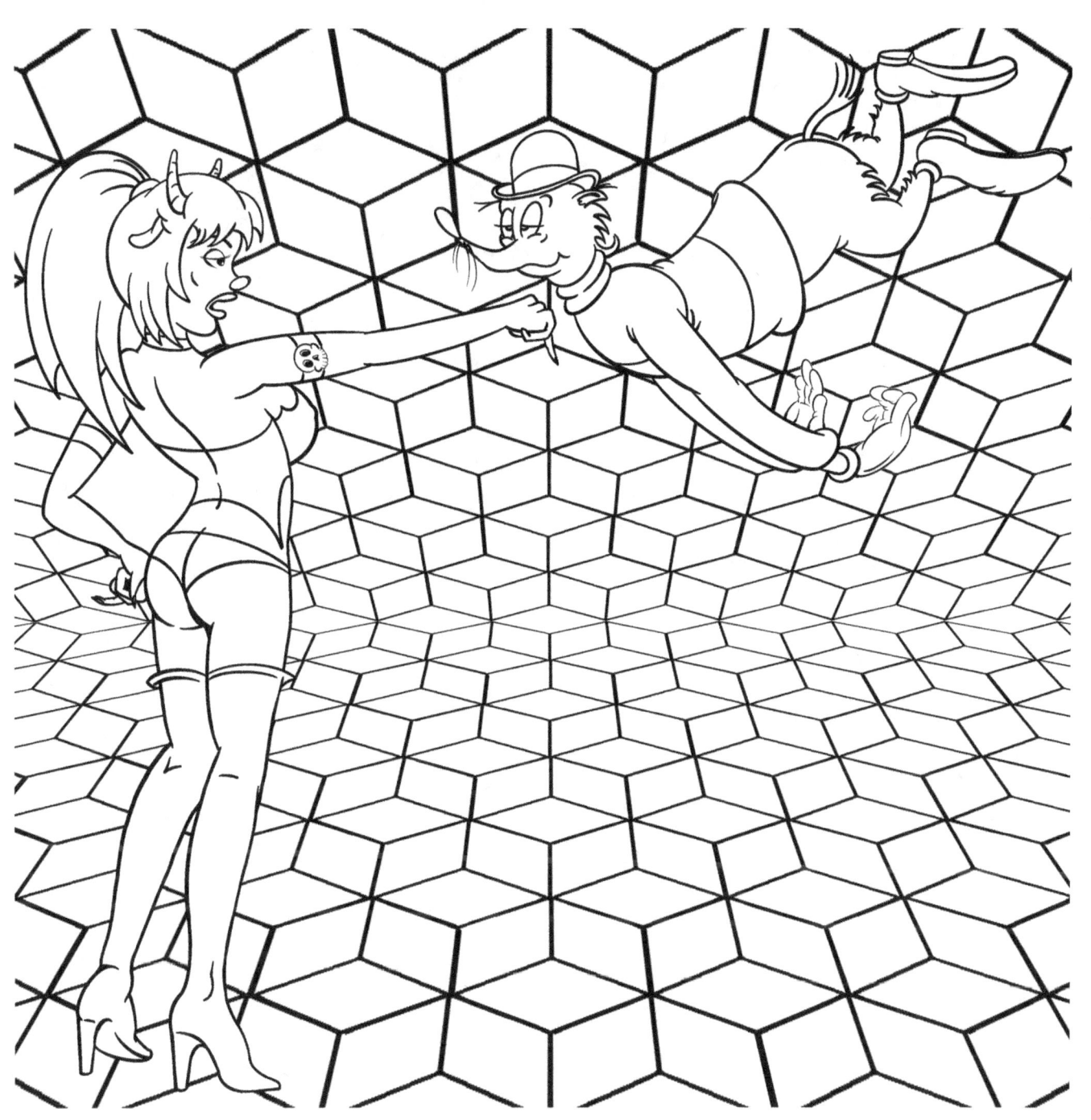

COME HERE!

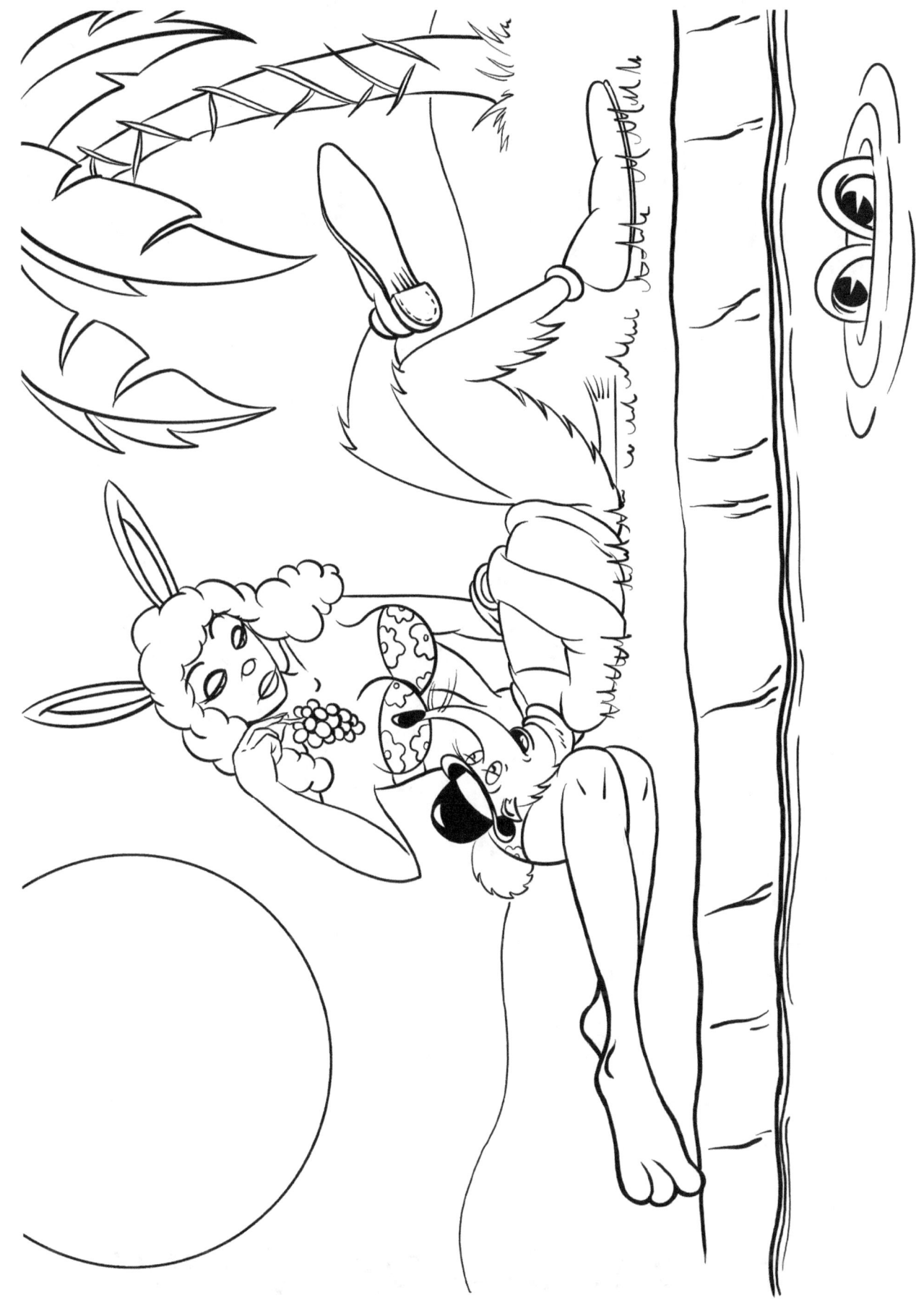

WILLY'S IDEA OF HEAVEN

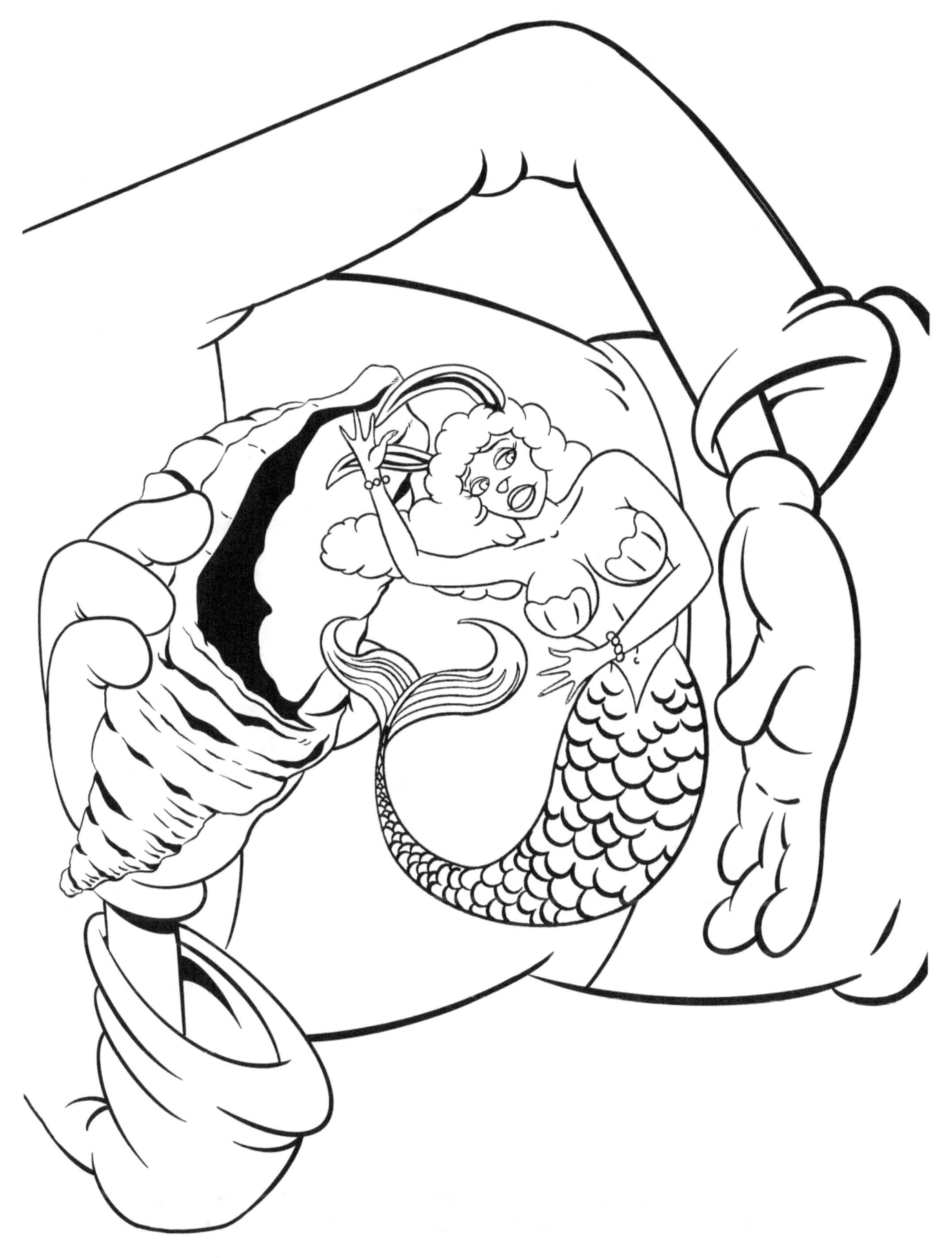

NICE CATCH OF THE DAY

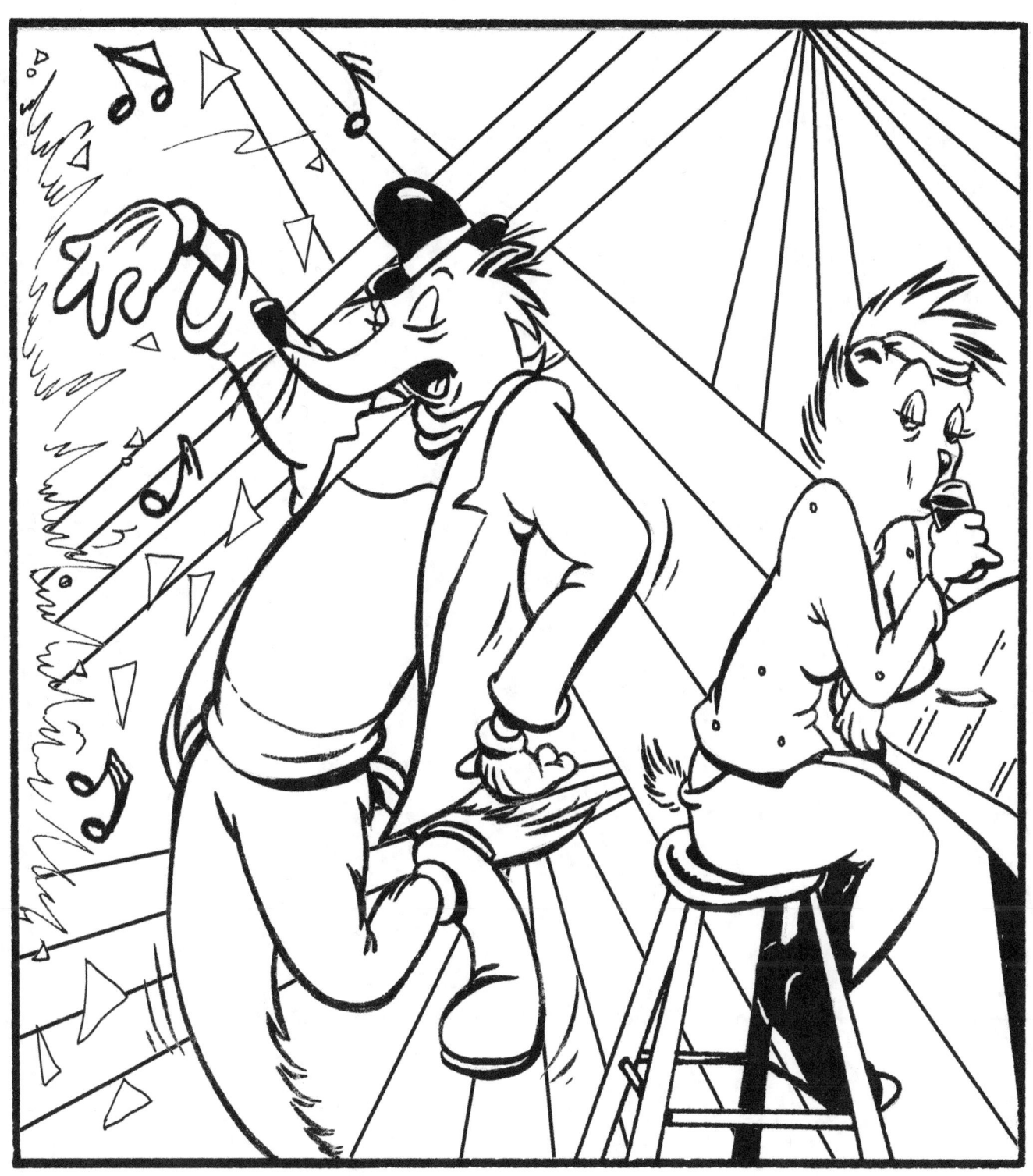

SAVE MY SEAT

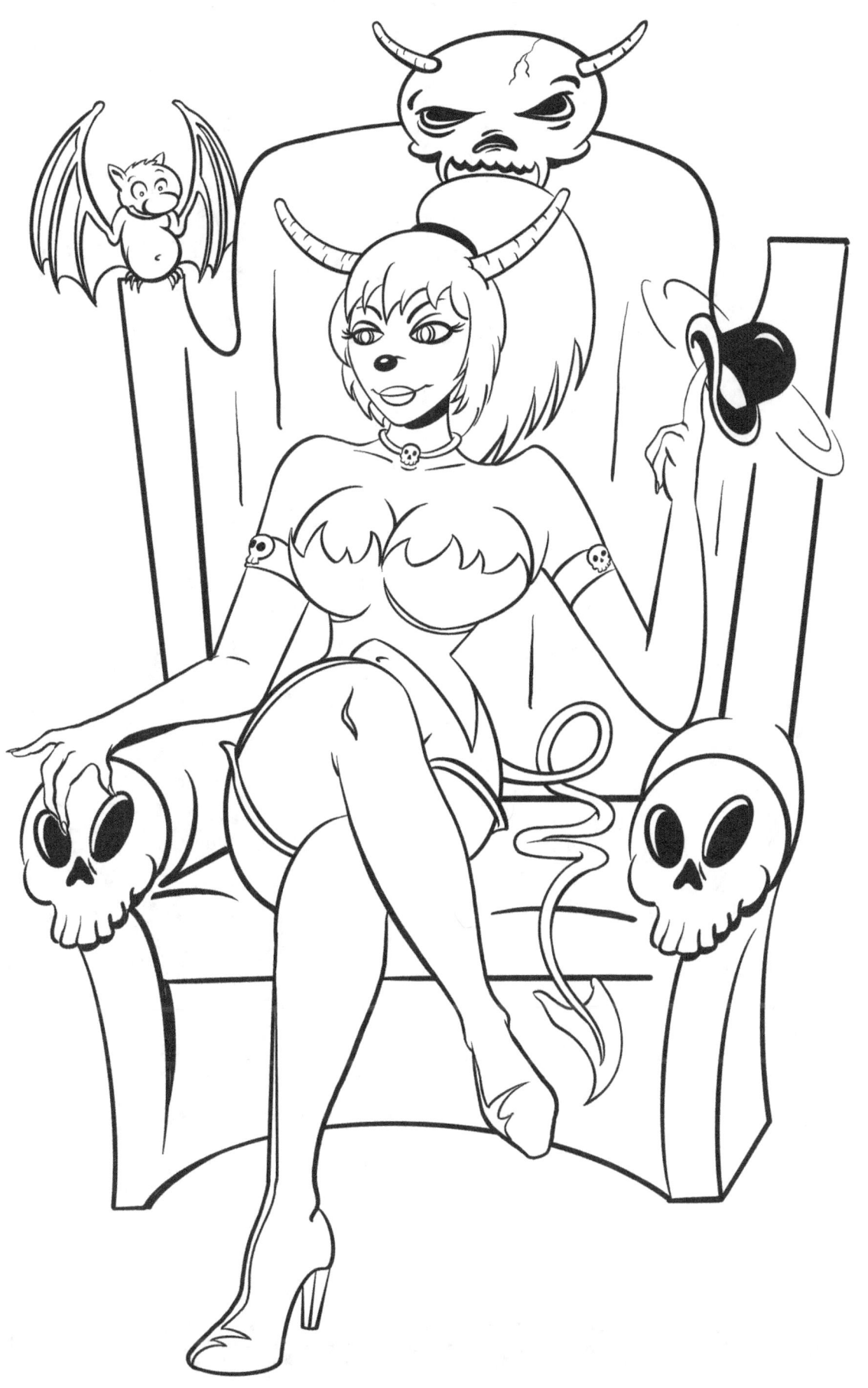

WANT IT? COME AND GET IT!

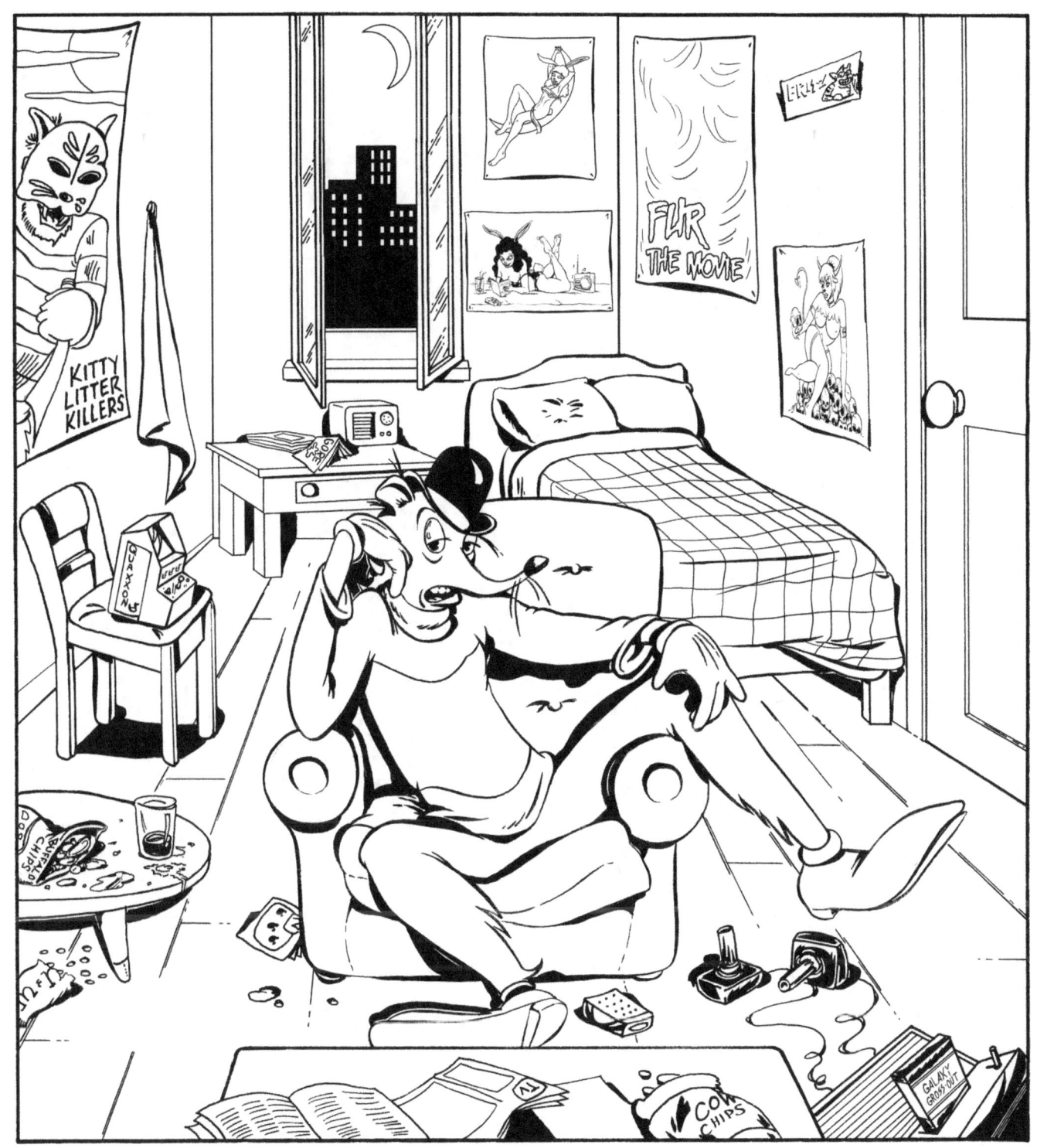

WILLY'S ROOM CIRCA 1984

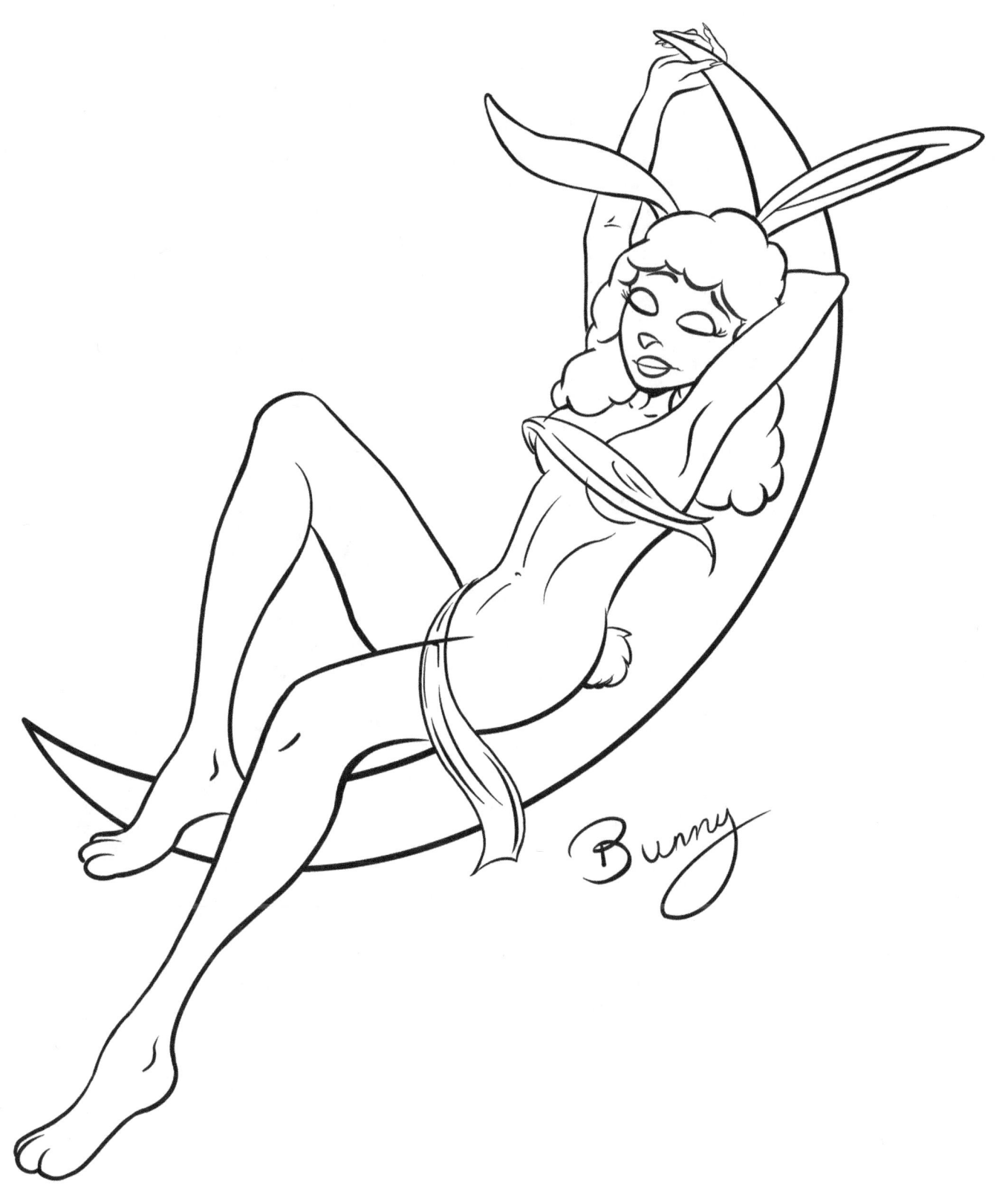

GOOD NIGHT

THERE'S EVEN MORE WILLY!

Read the comics that the coloring book is based on and finally figure out who these characters are that you spent time staying in the lines for! **Willy Weasely #1** is the book where Willy screws up the 80's. If you like mature-themed funny animal comics, wax nostalgic for the 80's, this is the comic for you. It was written and drawn in the 80's and first published in 2006. Look for it where you ordered this book... you know, the one you're holding now!

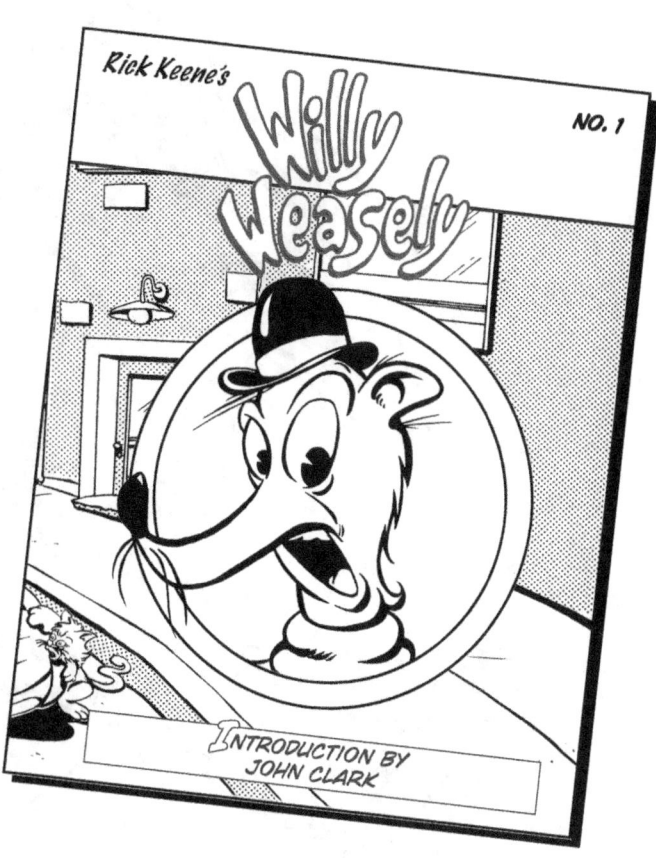

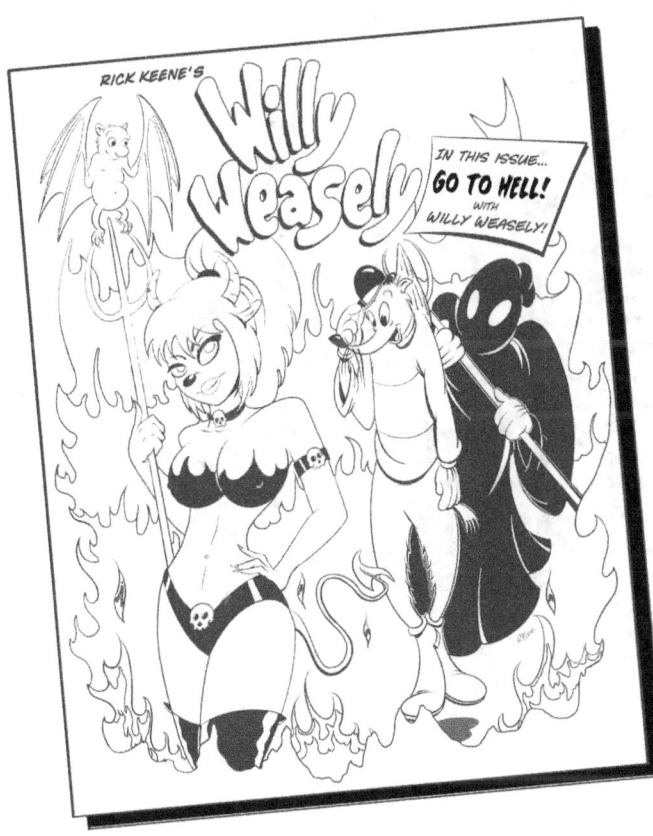

In **Go To Hell With Willy Weasely**, Willy goes to pay for his weasely behavior in life! The problem is, as if going to hell wasn't enough, Willy gets the hots for the devil and is clueless about how she wants him to pay! Another book for fans of funny animal mature-themed comics who like to read about characters that don't always make the right choices! Look for this comic where you ordered this book and go to hell... with Willy Weasely!

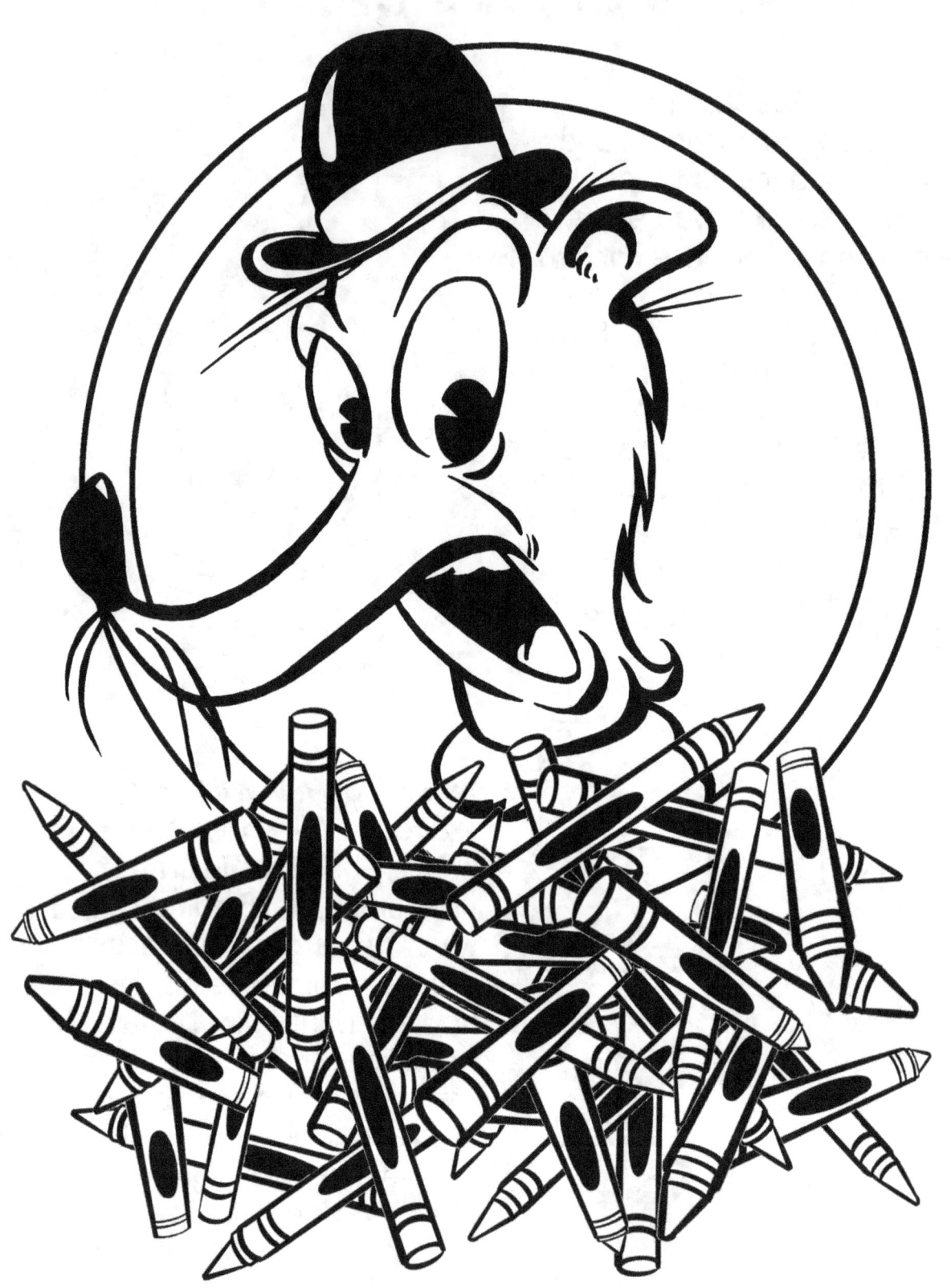

www.ingramcontent.com/pod-product-compliance
Lightning Source LLC
Chambersburg PA
CBHW081811240526
45465CB00032BA/2710